JULIAN ASS........

Julian Assange: A Biography of Truth,

Controversy, and the Fight for

Transparency

EVELYN JOHN

Table of contents

Introduction

Julian Assange, a name that evokes strong reactions and polarizing opinions, is a figure who has undeniably reshaped the landscape of modern journalism, transparency, and the discourse surrounding freedom of information. Born on July 3, 1971, in Townsville, Queensland, Australia, Assange has become synonymous with WikiLeaks, the controversial organization he founded in 2006. Through WikiLeaks, Assange has orchestrated some of the most significant leaks of classified information in recent history, challenging powerful governments and corporations and sparking global debates about secrecy, privacy, and the public's right to know.

Assange's journey from a curious and talented young hacker to a globally recognized (and often vilified) whistleblower and publisher is marked by dramatic episodes of legal battles, political asylum, and international intrigue. His early life, characterized by a nomadic childhood and an early exposure to computers, set the stage for his later endeavors. In the late 1980s, Assange was involved in hacking activities under the pseudonym "Mendax," a period during which he developed both his technical skills and a deep-seated belief in the importance of information freedom.

The creation of WikiLeaks in 2006 was a pivotal moment not just for Assange, but for journalism and global politics. The platform quickly became a repository for whistleblowers seeking to expose wrongdoing, offering a secure and anonymous way to leak documents. WikiLeaks gained international prominence with the release of the Collateral Murder video in 2010, which showed a U.S. helicopter attack in Baghdad that resulted in the deaths of multiple people, including two Reuters journalists. This was followed by the publication of the Afghan War Diary, the Iraq War Logs, and a vast trove of U.S. diplomatic cables. These disclosures, which provided unprecedented insights into the operations of the U.S. military and diplomatic corps, were both hailed for their contribution to public knowledge and condemned for their potential risks to national security and individual safety.

Assange's role in these high-profile leaks brought him under intense scrutiny from various governments, particularly the United States. In 2010, Sweden issued an arrest warrant for Assange over allegations of sexual misconduct, which he denied, claiming that the charges were politically motivated and part of a larger effort to extradite him to the U.S. In 2012, facing extradition to Sweden, Assange sought asylum in the Ecuadorian Embassy in London, where he remained confined for nearly seven years. This period was marked by a complex interplay of international law, diplomacy, and media scrutiny, as Assange continued to lead WikiLeaks from within the embassy.

The saga took another dramatic turn in April 2019, when Ecuador revoked Assange's asylum, leading to his arrest by British police. He was subsequently sentenced to prison for breaching bail conditions and faced an ongoing extradition battle with the United States. The U.S. government has charged Assange with multiple counts related to the publication of classified documents, including accusations under the Espionage Act. These charges have reignited fierce debates about press freedom, the role of whistleblowers, and the responsibilities of publishers in handling sensitive information.

Throughout his career, Assange has been a figure of both adulation and vilification. Supporters view him as a champion of transparency and a defender of the public's right to know, lauding his courage in exposing corruption and abuse of power. Critics, on the other hand, accuse him of recklessness, arguing that his actions have jeopardized national security, endangered lives, and strained diplomatic relations. This dichotomy is emblematic of the broader controversies surrounding WikiLeaks and the ethical implications of its operations.

Assange's impact extends beyond the immediate consequences of the leaks facilitated by WikiLeaks. His case has prompted significant legal and philosophical discussions about the nature of journalism in the digital age, the boundaries of free speech, and the accountability of governments and corporations. It has also highlighted the vulnerabilities and challenges faced by whistleblowers and the complex interplay between technology, law, and human rights.

In examining Julian Assange's life and legacy, one must navigate a landscape filled with legal intricacies, ethical dilemmas, and conflicting narratives. His story is not just about a man or an organization, but about the evolving dynamics of power, information, and public discourse in the 21st century. As Assange continues to fight his extradition and the charges against him, the debates he has ignited show no signs of abating, underscoring the enduring relevance and contentiousness of his contributions to the global stage.

Chapter 1

Early Life

Julian Assange, the enigmatic figure behind WikiLeaks, has had a profound impact on modern journalism and the transparency movement. His journey from a teenage hacker to a globally recognized whistleblower and publisher is a story marked by controversy, legal battles, and groundbreaking revelations. Born on July 3, 1971, in Townsville, Queensland, Australia, Assange exhibited an early interest in computers and hacking, which set the stage for his future endeavors.

Assange's initial foray into the world of hacking began in the late 1980s under the pseudonym "Mendax." His involvement in the hacking community led to allegations that he was part of the WANK (Worms Against Nuclear Killers) hack at NASA in 1989. Although never proven, Assange has referred to this event as the "origin of hacktivism." This sentiment was echoed in the Swedish television documentary WikiRebels, which hinted at his involvement. Assange's early hacking activities were also chronicled in the book Underground, where he served as a researcher.

In mid-1991, Assange and two other hackers began targeting MILNET, a data network used by the US military. Assange discovered reports suggesting internal hacking within the US military, and he claimed they had control over a backdoor in MILNET for two years. However, Ken Day, the former head of the Australian Federal Police's computer crime team, stated in 2012 that there was no evidence the International Subversives, the hacking group Assange was part of, had infiltrated MILNET. Day also noted that if Assange's claims were true, he could still face prosecution.

Assange created a program called Sycophant, which enabled the International Subversives to launch massive attacks on the US military. They regularly breached systems belonging to prominent entities within the US military-industrial complex and Australia's National University. At a security conference in Malaysia, Assange described himself as a famous teenage hacker, recounting how he had been reading generals' emails since he was 17. He attributed his motivation to his experiences with power during this period. The Australian Federal Police (AFP) launched Operation Weather, targeting the International Subversives. In September 1991, Assange was caught hacking into the Melbourne master terminal of Nortel, a Canadian telecommunications company. The AFP tapped Assange's phone line and raided his home, leading to his arrest. Assange faced 31 charges related to hacking, including defrauding Telecom Australia and obtaining unauthorized access to information. The prosecution argued that the

International Subversives' magazine encouraged others to hack, labeling it a "hacker's manual."

In May 1995, Assange's case was presented to the Supreme Court of Victoria, but it was sent back to the County Court. During this time, Assange fell into a deep depression, checking himself into a psychiatric hospital and spending six months in the wilderness around Melbourne. In December 1996, he struck a plea deal, pleading guilty to 24 hacking charges. The judge, noting Assange's disrupted childhood and lack of malicious intent, sentenced him to a fine and a good behavior bond.

Following his sentencing, Assange expressed his belief that he had been misled by the prosecution. Despite the judge's dismissal of his claims, this experience profoundly influenced Assange, steering him towards founding WikiLeaks.

In 1993, Assange assisted the Victoria Police Child Exploitation Unit in prosecuting individuals involved in child pornography. His role in aiding the police was highlighted during his 1996 sentencing for hacking charges. That same year, he took over the Suburbia Public Access Network, one of Australia's first public internet service providers. He joined the cypherpunk mailing list and focused on the information-sharing potential of the internet.

Assange began programming in 1994, developing network and encryption programs like the Rubberhose deniable encryption system and the Strobe port scanner. He also moderated the AUCRYPTO forum and ran a website offering computer security advice. Assange contributed research to Suelette Dreyfus's Underground, a book about Australian hackers, and co-founded Earthmen Technology, a company developing network intrusion detection technologies.

Throughout the 1990s, Assange facilitated leaks for activists and lawyers, acting as a conduit for leaked documents in the fight against local corruption. He and his mother formed the activist organization Parent Inquiry Into Child

Protection, using the Australian Freedom of Information Act to obtain documents and encourage insiders to come forward. An insider leaked a key departmental manual about custody dispute rules to the group.

In 1996, Assange mentioned a "LEAKS" project in emails to his lists, and in 1999, he registered the domain "leaks.org" but did not use it. He publicized a patent granted to the National Security Agency for voice-data harvesting technology, expressing concern over the potential for mass surveillance.

Chapter 2

WikiLeaks

In 2006, Julian Assange, along with a group of dissidents, mathematicians, and activists, founded WikiLeaks. Assange became a prominent member of its advisory board, dedicating himself to the cause with relentless fervor. Between 2007 and 2010, he traveled extensively across Africa, Asia, Europe, and North America to promote WikiLeaks and manage its operations.

WikiLeaks posted its first leak in December 2006, coinciding with the release of a five-page essay by Assange that detailed the philosophy behind the organization. This essay articulated a strategic vision where leaks would serve as a tool to compel organizations to curb abuses and dishonesty or suffer from what Assange termed a "secrecy tax." He explained that the more secretive and unjust an organization, the more leaks would incite fear and paranoia among its leadership, thereby hampering their efficiency and leading to a decline in their ability to maintain power.

Assange found crucial allies at the Chaos Computer Club conference in Berlin in December 2007, where he connected with key figures like Daniel Domscheit-Berg, Jacob Appelbaum, and the Swedish hosting company PRQ. These relationships bolstered WikiLeaks' infrastructure and expanded its network of volunteers and supporters.

During this period, Assange served as WikiLeaks' editor-in-chief and was one of its four permanent staff members. The organization also relied heavily on a larger pool of volunteers and experts. WikiLeaks began publishing internet censorship lists, leaks, and classified media from anonymous sources. Notable publications included revelations about drone strikes in Yemen, corruption in the Arab world, extrajudicial executions by Kenyan police, the 2008 Tibetan unrest in China, and the "Petrogate" oil scandal in Peru. These disclosures had a significant impact on political discourse in numerous countries and across various issues.

From its inception, WikiLeaks aimed to collaborate with established media outlets to amplify its impact. The organization developed strong relationships with parts of the German and British press. A notable collaboration with Sunday Times journalist Jon Swain on political killings in Kenya garnered public recognition and won Assange the 2009 Amnesty International New Media Award. The Kenya leak led to widespread outrage and political upheaval, making corruption a major issue in the subsequent election, which was marred by violence. According to Assange, this exposure of corruption was necessary despite the ensuing turmoil, as it provided the Kenyan public with crucial information.

WikiLeaks' profile soared in 2008 when the Swiss bank, Bank Julius Baer, attempted to block the publication of its internal documents through a Californian court injunction. Assange criticized financial institutions for operating outside the rule of law and received substantial support from free-speech and civil rights groups. The bank's attempt to suppress the information backfired, drawing global attention to both WikiLeaks and the documents in question due to the Streisand effect.

By 2009, WikiLeaks had achieved significant success in exposing powerful entities and advocating for freedom of speech. However, Assange's goal of crowd-sourcing document analysis did not fully materialize, and many leaks did not attract the mainstream media attention he had hoped for.

In July 2009, WikiLeaks released the full report of a commission of inquiry into corruption in the Turks and Caicos Islands, which had been established by the British Foreign and Commonwealth Office. The report had been suppressed by an injunction obtained by those named in it. WikiLeaks managed to obtain and publish the complete text, revealing that foreign property developers had made substantial payments and secret loans to senior politicians, including the former premier, Michael Misick.

Assange's work through WikiLeaks has had profound ramifications, exposing systemic corruption, human rights abuses, and other forms of misconduct. The organization's disclosures have forced governments and institutions to confront their actions and have fostered greater accountability.

Julian Assange's journey with WikiLeaks is a testament to the power of information in the digital age. Despite facing numerous legal challenges, including a prolonged asylum in the Ecuadorian Embassy in London and ongoing extradition battles, Assange has remained steadfast in his commitment to transparency and the public's right to know. His actions have sparked global debates about the balance between transparency and security, the role of whistleblowers, and the ethical responsibilities of those who publish sensitive information.

Assange's influence extends beyond the immediate impacts of the leaks. His work has inspired a new generation of activists, journalists, and technologists dedicated to uncovering the truth and holding the powerful to account. The controversies and legal battles surrounding Assange and WikiLeaks continue to shape discussions about press freedom, government transparency, and the future of investigative journalism.

The leaks provided by Chelsea Manning to WikiLeaks, encompassing the Cablegate, Iraq War, and Afghan War documents, had profound global repercussions, influencing diplomacy and shaping public opinion across different regions. These leaks revealed extensive details about U.S. military operations and diplomatic communications, leading to widespread debate and controversy.

The U.S. government pointed to chat logs between Manning and a person believed to be Julian Assange as crucial evidence in their indictment against Assange in 2018.

These logs were central to their claim that Assange had actively collaborated with Manning. Manning, during her court martial, disclosed that she communicated with a WikiLeaks associate through a secure chat, discussing various classified files, including those from Guantanamo Bay.

In these exchanges, Manning inquired if Assange could assist in decrypting passwords using LM hash cracking techniques. Assange responded affirmatively, suggesting the use of rainbow tables—a method used by WikiLeaks to crack hashes and uncover passwords. An affidavit from an FBI agent argued that this demonstrated an "illegal agreement" to aid in password cracking, which was pivotal to the prosecution's case against Assange.

During her court martial, Manning testified that her decision to download detainee assessment briefs (DABs) from Guantanamo Bay followed a conversation with a WikiLeaks associate. Manning believed that while Assange did not view the DABs as politically significant, he thought they could contribute to the historical narrative of Guantanamo's operations. This conversation influenced Manning to proceed with the data download, underscoring the collaborative aspect of her interactions with WikiLeaks.

In 2011, a series of events led to the unintentional exposure of a WikiLeaks file containing U.S. diplomatic cables. The chain of events began in August 2010, when Assange provided Guardian journalist David Leigh with an encryption key and URL to access the file. In February 2011, Leigh and Luke Harding published the encryption key in their book "WikiLeaks: Inside Julian Assange's War on Secrecy," mistakenly believing it was temporary.

Following cyber-attacks on WikiLeaks in December 2010, supporters mirrored the encrypted files across various sites. Once WikiLeaks realized the risk, they informed the U.S. State Department. The situation escalated when the German magazine Der Freitag published details in August

2011 that enabled people to reconstruct the information. On September 1, 2011, WikiLeaks decided to make the unredacted cables publicly accessible and searchable.

WikiLeaks' decision to publish the unredacted cables was met with condemnation from its media partners, including The Guardian. These partners criticized Assange for the unilateral decision, arguing it endangered lives and compromised sensitive information. However, journalist Glenn Greenwald defended the move, stating that releasing the cables in full ensured equal access to the information and allowed protective measures to be taken for sources.

The U.S. government's response included establishing an Information Review Task Force (IRTF) to assess the leaks' impact. The IRTF, involving up to 125 personnel over ten months, reported that the leaks could cause "serious damage" and endanger U.S. sources. However, during Chelsea Manning's sentencing, Brigadier General Robert Carr, head of the IRTF, admitted that no lives were lost as a direct result of WikiLeaks' publications, a point that significantly weakened the argument that the leaks had caused fatalities.

The U.S. government has persistently sought Assange's extradition, arguing that his actions endangered lives. Despite these assertions, during Assange's 2020 extradition hearings, the U.S. Justice Department conceded that they had not identified any individuals harmed directly due to the disclosures. John Young, operator of the website Cryptome, testified that his site had published the unredacted cables a day before WikiLeaks, highlighting that the information was already accessible online.

Assange's defense presented evidence aimed at demonstrating his efforts to protect lives. They argued that Assange took considerable measures to redact sensitive information and mitigate risks to individuals. The legal battles surrounding Assange and WikiLeaks continue to evoke discussions about the balance between transparency and security, the role of whistleblowers, and the ethics of publishing classified information.

In December 2010, PostFinance, a Swiss bank, announced the closure of Julian Assange's account, citing that Assange had provided false information about his place of residence when opening the account. Although this action had "no criminal consequences," it significantly impacted WikiLeaks. The account was intended for donations to the Julian Assange and WikiLeaks Staff Defence Fund. WikiLeaks condemned the closure, suggesting it was part of a broader financial blockade against the organization.

In 2010, leaked documents from WikiLeaks included an unsigned letter purportedly from Assange, authorizing Israel Shamir to apply for a Russian visa on his behalf. WikiLeaks denied that Assange had ever applied for such a visa or authored the letter. However, reports from The New York Times revealed that Assange had considered seeking refuge in Russia as early as November 2010, and by January 2011, Russia had indeed issued him a visa.

During the 2011 Egyptian revolution, when then-President Hosni Mubarak attempted to shut down mobile phone networks to stifle protests, Assange and WikiLeaks took action. Andrew O'Hagan reported that Assange, alongside other WikiLeaks associates, hacked into Nortel's systems to counteract Mubarak's efforts, effectively reversing the network shutdown imposed by the regime.

In the subsequent years, WikiLeaks continued to release high-profile documents, significantly impacting global political discourse. Among these were the Guantanamo Bay files leak, the Syria Files, the Kissinger Cables, and the Saudi Cables.

The Guantanamo Bay files leak, published by WikiLeaks, consisted of classified documents detailing the operations and detainee assessments of the Guantanamo Bay detention camp. These documents provided a comprehensive view of the treatment of detainees and the U.S. government's rationale for their detention, sparking international debates on human rights and U.S. foreign policy.

The Syria Files, released by WikiLeaks, contained over two million emails from Syrian political figures, ministries, and associated companies. This trove of information exposed the inner workings of the Syrian government and its dealings with various international entities, offering insights into the political and economic landscape of Syria during a tumultuous period.

The Kissinger Cables, another significant release, consisted of more than 1.7 million U.S. diplomatic records from 1973 to 1976. These documents, associated with former U.S. Secretary of State Henry Kissinger, shed light on U.S. foreign policy decisions and diplomatic communications during a critical period of the Cold War, revealing previously unknown details about U.S. interactions with other nations.

In 2015, WikiLeaks published the Saudi Cables, which included over half a million documents from the Saudi Foreign Ministry. These documents provided a rare glimpse into the kingdom's diplomatic activities, internal communications, and foreign relations strategies, highlighting the complexities of Saudi Arabia's role in regional and global politics.

As of July 2015, Assange claimed that WikiLeaks had published more than ten million documents and associated analyses. He described this vast collection as "a giant library of the world's most persecuted documents." This repository of information encompasses a wide range of topics, from government corruption and corporate malfeasance to human rights violations and political scandals.

WikiLeaks' activities have had a profound impact on global journalism, transparency, and the public's right to know. By making classified and sensitive information accessible, WikiLeaks has challenged traditional power structures and pushed the boundaries of investigative journalism. The organization's releases have led to increased scrutiny of governments and corporations, prompting discussions on accountability and ethical governance.

Throughout this period, Assange's legal and political struggles have been a focal point of public attention. Facing extradition attempts, legal battles, and accusations of espionage, Assange's situation has sparked debates on press freedom, whistleblower protections, and the limits of state power. His supporters view him as a champion of transparency and free speech, while critics argue that his actions have endangered lives and compromised national security.

The legacy of WikiLeaks continues to evolve as new developments unfold. The organization's impact on the dissemination of information and the public's ability to access it remains a contentious and significant aspect of contemporary political and journalistic landscapes. As the world grapples with issues of privacy, security, and the free flow of information, WikiLeaks' contributions to these debates will undoubtedly be remembered and analyzed for years to come.

Chapter 3

Legal Issues

In 2010, Julian Assange faced legal proceedings in the United Kingdom regarding a request for his extradition to Sweden. This request stemmed from a preliminary investigation into allegations of sexual offenses that were made in August 2010 while Assange was in Sweden.

Assange left Sweden for the UK on September 27, 2010, and was arrested in his absence the same day. The accusations included rape of a lesser degree, unlawful coercion, and multiple instances of sexual molestation. Assange had initially planned to return to Stockholm for a police interview on October 14, 2010, but ultimately decided against it. His request for a Swedish residency permit was denied on October 18, 2010, due to his application not meeting all the requirements.

On November 18, 2010, Swedish Director of Public Prosecution Marianne Ny ordered Assange's detention on suspicion of rape, three cases of sexual molestation, and unlawful coercion. The Stockholm District Court issued a European Arrest Warrant, which was subsequently appealed to the Svea Court of Appeal. The appeal resulted in the charges being adjusted to suspicion of rape of a lesser degree, unlawful coercion, and two cases of sexual molestation. The Supreme Court of Sweden decided not to hear Assange's case, leaving the European Arrest Warrant in place.

On November 30, 2010, Interpol issued a Red Notice, placing Assange on its most-wanted list. Assange surrendered to the Metropolitan Police Extradition Unit in London on December 7, 2010, and was remanded to Wandsworth Prison. Upon his arrest, he refused to cooperate with standard procedures such as providing photographs, fingerprints, and DNA samples.

Assange was granted bail on December 16, 2010, with conditions including residence at Ellingham Hall in Norfolk and wearing an electronic tag. The bail was set at £240,000, with a deposit of £200,000. Upon his release, Assange expressed his intention to continue his work and protest his innocence, labeling the extradition proceedings as part of a smear campaign. He suggested that the Swedish case was an attempt to extradite him to the United States, a claim denied by Swedish prosecutors.

On August 12, 2015, Swedish prosecutors announced that the statute of limitations had expired for three of the allegations against Assange while he was residing in the Ecuadorian embassy. On May 19, 2017, the investigation into the rape allegation was dropped due to Assange's asylum. Throughout these proceedings, Assange maintained that he feared extradition to the United States if he were sent to Sweden.

In May 2019, the Swedish Prosecution Authority reopened the investigation against Assange, expressing the intent to extradite him from the UK after he served a 50-week prison sentence for skipping bail. However, in June 2019, the Uppsala District Court denied a request to detain Assange, thus preventing his extradition to Sweden. By November 19, 2019, Swedish prosecutors dropped the case entirely, citing that the evidence had significantly weakened due to the elapsed time, although they remained confident in the complainant's account.

The allegations and subsequent legal battles significantly impacted Assange's life and WikiLeaks' operations. Assange's claim that the extradition attempts were politically motivated brought international attention and debate over the intersection of legal proceedings, political asylum, and freedom of information. The prolonged legal struggles underscored the complexities of international law, extradition treaties, and the protections afforded to individuals under asylum.

Throughout this period, Assange's supporters argued that the charges were a pretext to facilitate his extradition to the United States, where he faced potential charges related to WikiLeaks' publication of classified information. This perspective highlighted concerns over press freedom and the treatment of whistleblowers and activists by powerful governments.

Following WikiLeaks' release of material provided by Chelsea Manning, U.S. authorities initiated an investigation into both WikiLeaks and its founder, Julian Assange, under the Espionage Act of 1917. In November 2010, U.S. Attorney General Eric Holder confirmed the existence of "an active, ongoing criminal investigation" into WikiLeaks. Legal documents revealed that WikiLeaks was under scrutiny by a federal grand jury in Alexandria, Virginia, and that the U.S. government was urging its allies to launch criminal investigations against Assange.

In 2010, the FBI informed Assange's lawyer that he was not the subject of an investigation. Despite this, the NSA added Assange to its "Manhunting Timeline," which tracked efforts to capture or eliminate alleged terrorists. In 2011, the NSA considered categorizing WikiLeaks as a "malicious foreign actor" to justify extensive surveillance. That same year, WikiLeaks volunteer Sigurdur Thordarson became the FBI's first informant within the organization, providing them with several hard drives copied from Assange and other core WikiLeaks members.

In December 2011, during the Chelsea Manning case, prosecutors disclosed chat logs between Manning and someone they identified as Assange. Assange denied knowing the identities of WikiLeaks' sources, asserting that communications with sources were anonymous. He dismissed allegations that WikiLeaks had conspired with

Manning as "absolute nonsense," maintaining that the organization only learned Manning's name from media reports. Despite this, the chat logs were presented as evidence during Manning's court-martial in 2013, where the prosecution argued that WikiLeaks had helped Manning reverse-engineer a password. Manning testified that she acted alone and was not pressured by anyone from WikiLeaks to provide more information.

In 2012, diplomatic cables between Australia and the United States revealed that the U.S. government was considering a wide range of charges against Assange, including espionage and conspiracy. U.S. diplomats dismissed claims that the investigation was politically motivated and emphasized that Manning had been influenced by WikiLeaks' list of "most wanted" leaks. In 2013, U.S. officials suggested it was unlikely that the Justice Department would indict Assange for publishing classified documents, as it would also necessitate prosecuting news organizations and journalists who published similar material.

Despite the Obama administration's reluctance to indict Assange due to insufficient evidence distinguishing his actions from those of journalists, the Trump administration intensified efforts to prosecute him. CIA Director Mike Pompeo and Attorney General Jeff Sessions pursued Assange more aggressively, aiming to uncover WikiLeaks' connections with Russian intelligence. Law enforcement officials even considered offering Assange immunity in exchange for his testimony, but negotiations ceased following the Vault 7 disclosures, which detailed CIA hacking tools.

In April 2017, U.S. officials prepared to file formal charges against Assange. His indictment was unsealed in 2019 and expanded upon later that year and in 2020. Legal scholar Steve Vladeck noted that prosecutors likely accelerated the case due to the impending statute of limitations on

Assange's most significant leaks. The Mueller report, released in early 2019, indicated that the Special Counsel's office had considered charging WikiLeaks or Assange as conspirators in a computer-intrusion conspiracy. However, "factual uncertainties" about Assange's role in the hacks or their distribution remained under investigation by the U.S. Attorney's Office.

On September 2, 2011, Australian Attorney General Robert McClelland issued a statement addressing the legal ramifications of WikiLeaks' publication of U.S. diplomatic cables. McClelland revealed that among the documents released by WikiLeaks was information that could potentially identify an Australian Security Intelligence Organisation (ASIO) officer. Under Australian law, publishing information that could expose the identity of intelligence personnel is considered a serious offense.

McClelland noted that while WikiLeaks had previously taken measures to redact identifying details to protect individuals and national security, it appeared that such precautions had not been applied to the documents released in that particular week. This lapse, he suggested, could place Julian Assange in legal jeopardy in Australia. Both The Guardian and Al Jazeera reported that this development meant Assange might face prosecution if he returned to Australia.

In 2014, WikiLeaks found itself at the center of another legal controversy in Australia. The organization published information regarding allegations of political bribery, which was in direct violation of a gag order imposed by Australian authorities. The gag order had been designed to prevent the dissemination of sensitive information related to ongoing investigations. This breach of the order brought WikiLeaks back into the spotlight and intensified scrutiny of Assange and his organization.

Peter Bartlett, an Australian media lawyer, commented on the situation, noting that while WikiLeaks operated from outside Australia's jurisdiction, any future return of Assange to Australia would likely result in charges related to the violation of suppression orders. Bartlett's insight underscored the legal complexities faced by Assange, highlighting the potential consequences if he were to step foot back on Australian soil.

The legal landscape for Assange and WikiLeaks in Australia involves intricate considerations of national security, freedom of information, and the legal limits on media reporting. The tension between protecting state secrets and upholding the public's right to information continues to be a central theme in the ongoing legal battles surrounding Assange and his organization. As legal proceedings and public debates evolve, the intersection of law, journalism, and international diplomacy remains a critical area of scrutiny.

Chapter 4

Ecuadorian embassy period

In December 2010, Renata Avila, a Guatemalan human rights lawyer, advised Julian Assange to "plan an escape and reimburse his supporters for the bail money." This advice came amidst growing legal pressures. By June 19, 2012, Ecuadorian Foreign Minister Ricardo Patiño announced that Assange had sought political asylum and was residing at the Ecuadorian embassy in London. The embassy converted an office into a makeshift apartment, outfitting it with essentials such as a bed, a telephone, a sun lamp, a computer, a shower, a treadmill, and a kitchenette. To accommodate Assange's need for privacy and quiet, the embassy staff even removed the toilet from the women's bathroom so he could sleep undisturbed.

Assange's living space was modest, roughly 30 square meters (320 square feet), and his diet consisted mainly of takeaways and meals prepared by embassy staff. Despite these accommodations, Assange's decision to take refuge in the embassy rather than face court proceedings meant he was in violation of his bail conditions. This led to his supporters, including prominent figures like journalist Jemima Goldsmith, forfeiting £200,000 in bail money and £40,000 in sureties. Goldsmith, initially surprised by Assange's decision to seek asylum, expressed a desire for him to face the allegations in Sweden but acknowledged his fear of potential extradition to the U.S.

The UK government responded to the asylum request by notifying the Ecuadorian authorities that British law allowed them to arrest Assange within the embassy. However, Ecuadorian officials, including Patiño, perceived this as a breach of the Vienna Convention, which protects diplomatic missions from such intrusions. From June 2012 to October 2015, the Metropolitan Police Service maintained a constant presence outside the embassy, with officers stationed there to detain Assange if he left the premises. The policing operation, which was eventually scaled back due to cost considerations, had a reported expense of £12.6 million. Although the officers were withdrawn, the police stated they would continue employing various tactics to apprehend Assange if he attempted to leave.

Amidst these developments, Australian authorities took a cautious stance. Attorney-General Nicola Roxon informed Assange's lawyer that Australia would not involve itself in international discussions regarding Assange's future. Prime Minister Julia Gillard asserted that there was no evidence of an imminent U.S. indictment against Assange at that time. Roxon suggested that should Assange be imprisoned in the U.S., he could apply for an international prisoner transfer to Australia. Assange's legal team interpreted this response as a "declaration of abandonment," reflecting his belief that the Australian government had effectively distanced itself from his plight. WikiLeaks insiders further suggested that this perceived abandonment influenced Assange's decision to seek asylum.

On August 16, 2012, Ecuador officially granted Assange political asylum, citing fears that the U.S. secret investigation posed a significant threat to his safety. Ecuador's statement highlighted Assange's staunch defense of freedom of expression and press, asserting that his continued presence in the embassy was necessary to protect his life and personal integrity. Ecuadorian President Rafael Correa confirmed on August 18 that Assange could remain at the embassy indefinitely.

In December 2012, documents revealed that Australia had no objections to a potential U.S. extradition request and that Assange had declined an offer of consular assistance. Despite his confined circumstances, Assange expressed a sense of liberation within the embassy, viewing his confinement as a self-imposed protective measure rather than an imprisonment.

In 2013, WikiLeaks played a pivotal role in aiding whistleblower Edward Snowden in his escape from U.S. law enforcement. Following the revocation of Snowden's passport by the U.S., leaving him stranded in Russia, WikiLeaks explored options for his safe transport to South America. They considered using the presidential jet of a sympathetic South American leader, though they initially mentioned Bolivian President Evo Morales's jet to mislead U.S. authorities. In July 2013, Morales's plane was forced to land in Austria after the U.S. exerted pressure on Italy, France, and Spain to deny the jet access to their airspace, based on false rumors that Snowden was aboard.

Assange commented on the incident, arguing that the grounding of Morales's jet demonstrated the extent of U.S. influence over Western European countries, asserting that a mere phone call from U.S. intelligence was sufficient to close off airspace to a diplomatic flight. Assange advised Snowden that staying in Russia was safer compared to other potential destinations such as Venezuela, Brazil, or Ecuador, which were perceived as less secure.

In 2015, Bolivia's ambassador to Russia, Maria Luisa Ramos, accused Assange of jeopardizing Morales's safety. Assange responded with regret, acknowledging the unforeseen nature of international responses but standing by his assessment that he could not predict such extreme measures by other countries.

Chapter 5

Political positions

In the 2013 Australian federal election, Julian Assange ran as a candidate for the Australian Senate representing Victoria and founded the WikiLeaks Party to support his campaign. Despite his efforts, Assange did not secure a seat in the Senate. His decision to run was influenced by the public criticism directed at WikiLeaks by then-Prime Minister Julia Gillard. Assange suggested that his candidacy was partially motivated by a belief that winning a Senate seat could pressure the U.S. to terminate its grand jury investigation into him, and potentially compel the British government to cease its pursuit due to the political repercussions.

Assange's statement was seen as an indication that one of his primary objectives in running for office was to leverage political influence to halt the ongoing investigations. He described himself as a libertarian and expressed a commitment to using parliamentary privilege to counteract gag orders imposed by the courts. Additionally, Assange articulated a vision of protecting individuals and small businesses from the overreach of large corporations and government entities. He also acknowledged the complexity of moral and social issues such as euthanasia and same-sex marriage, suggesting that these topics had valid arguments on all sides.

However, the WikiLeaks Party faced internal conflicts regarding its governance and electoral strategy. Notably, a controversial preference deal in 2013 led to significant discord within the party. Leaked emails revealed that Assange was instrumental in negotiating this deal, which included attempts to grant himself veto powers and transform the party's internal National Council into a mere formality for decisions made by individual candidates. Assange also proposed that he should assume the presidency of the party, a position not specified in the party's constitution.

Following the 2013 election, Assange expressed his intention to run for a Senate seat again in three to six years and indicated that the WikiLeaks Party would persist. Although he initially planned to stand for election in the 2014 special election in Western Australia, the Australian Electoral Commission ruled him ineligible. By 2015, the party was deregistered due to insufficient membership. Assange claimed that Bank of America had blocked donations intended for the WikiLeaks Party, which he suggested contributed to its difficulties.

In 2012 and 2013, Edward Snowden's disclosures revealed that the New Zealand government was involved in creating a covert mass surveillance program named "Operation Speargun." On September 15, 2014, during his campaign efforts for Kim Dotcom, Assange appeared via remote video link at a town hall meeting in Auckland to discuss the program. During this appearance, Assange referenced the Snowden documents to assert that he himself had been targeted by "Operation Speargun," describing it as an embodiment of a troubling and Orwellian surveillance future being secretly developed in New Zealand.

Assange's involvement in Dotcom's campaign was notable for its focus on surveillance and privacy issues, reflecting broader concerns about government overreach and the erosion of civil liberties. His statements highlighted the growing global debate over surveillance practices and their implications for personal freedoms, reinforcing his ongoing commitment to privacy advocacy and transparency.

In 2014, a company hired to monitor Julian Assange raised alarms to the Ecuadorian government, suggesting that he was "intercepting and gathering information from the embassy and the people who worked there." This included compromising the embassy's communication systems, an allegation WikiLeaks dismissed as "an anonymous libel aligned with the current UK-US government onslaught against Mr Assange." El País reported that a November 2014 UC Global report found a briefcase with a listening device in a room used by Assange. This incident reinforced suspicions that Assange was eavesdropping on diplomatic personnel, including the ambassador, to gain privileged information and maintain his status within the embassy. Ambassador Falconí noted that Assange was evasive when questioned about the briefcase.

On July 3, 2015, Paris newspaper Le Monde published an open letter from Assange to French President François Hollande, urging the French government to grant him refugee status. Hollande's response was curt, stating, "France cannot act on his request. The situation of Mr Assange does not present an immediate danger."

In September 2016 and again on January 12, 2017, WikiLeaks tweeted that if President Obama granted Chelsea Manning clemency, Assange would agree to US extradition. After Obama commuted Manning's sentence on January 17, 2017, he clarified that Assange's offer had not influenced the decision. Nonetheless, WikiLeaks tweeted that Assange remained "still happy" to agree to extradition if his rights were respected. Assange argued that Obama's decision to grant clemency to Manning was a strategic move to "make life hard" for him and undermine his credibility. Melinda Taylor, one of WikiLeaks' lawyers, confirmed that Assange would honor his offer, reiterating that he stood by his commitment to face extradition under the specified conditions.

Despite these statements, Assange faced considerable pressure to agree to extradition but ultimately reneged on his offer. WikiLeaks' lawyers, Melinda Taylor and Barry Pollack, contended that the clemency did not meet

Assange's conditions, arguing that Manning should have been released immediately.

On May 19, 2017, Assange appeared on the embassy's balcony, announcing to a gathered crowd that, despite the cessation of the Swedish sex investigation, he would continue to stay inside the embassy to avoid extradition to the United States. During his prolonged stay, Assange received numerous visitors, including notable personalities such as Pamela Anderson. Anderson recounted her visits, saying, "I visited Julian regularly at the Ecuadorian embassy in London, staying for hours at a time. He looked forward to the vegan meals I'd bring him, and he was intrigued by my perspective on global issues. Most of his visitors were lawyers, politicians, and people he worked with closely on legal matters. My presence was different, maybe a little refreshing, human. Somewhat stimulating for him."

The interactions Assange had while at the embassy were marked by a constant tension between his need for asylum and the diplomatic and legal challenges surrounding his case. The revelations by the monitoring company highlighted the intricate web of surveillance and counter-surveillance that characterized Assange's life in the embassy. The discovery of the briefcase with the listening device added another layer of complexity, suggesting an environment fraught with mistrust and espionage.

The French government's refusal to grant Assange refugee status was a significant blow, reflecting the broader international hesitancy to intervene in Assange's situation. Hollande's succinct dismissal underscored the diplomatic tightrope that many nations walked regarding Assange, balancing international law, domestic politics, and their relationships with the United States.

Assange's conditional offer to face US extradition in exchange for Manning's clemency was a calculated risk. It was a move designed to draw attention to the perceived injustices he faced while also highlighting Manning's plight.

However, the subsequent political maneuvers and Assange's eventual backtrack on the offer illustrated the unpredictable and often contradictory nature of his legal and diplomatic strategies.

Pamela Anderson's visits provided a glimpse into the more personal and human side of Assange's confinement. Her accounts painted a picture of a man who, despite his controversial status, sought solace and normalcy in small gestures of kindness and intellectual engagement. Her description of her visits as "refreshing" and "stimulating" for Assange emphasized the isolating and high-stakes nature of his life in the embassy.

On July 22, 2016, WikiLeaks released a cache of emails and documents from the Democratic National Committee (DNC), revealing internal communications that appeared to show the DNC favoring Hillary Clinton over her primary rival, Bernie Sanders. The leaked documents suggested that the DNC was considering various strategies to undermine Sanders' campaign. This controversial release led to the resignation of DNC chairwoman Debbie Wasserman Schultz and prompted the DNC to issue a formal apology to Sanders.

The timing of the release was strategically chosen to coincide with the 2016 Democratic National Convention. The New York Times reported that Julian Assange, the founder of WikiLeaks, had orchestrated the release at this particular moment because he believed Clinton had advocated for his indictment and viewed her as a "liberal war hawk." Assange's actions were seen as an attempt to influence the Democratic primaries by exposing internal party biases and machinations.

On October 7, 2016, WikiLeaks began publishing a series of emails from John Podesta, Clinton's campaign chairman. This release added to the ongoing controversy surrounding the Clinton campaign and was perceived as another strategic move by Assange. Shortly thereafter, the Ecuadorian government cut off Assange's internet access from October 15 until December, citing concerns about election interference. Surveillance reports later indicated that, on October 19, associates of Assange removed several boxes covered with blankets and around 100 hard drives from the embassy where Assange was residing.

In November 2017, WikiLeaks reached out to Donald Trump Jr., asking him to share a tweet with a fabricated quote allegedly from Hillary Clinton saying, "Can't we just drone this guy?" This quote had been falsely attributed to Clinton by the website True Pundit. Following the 2016 election, WikiLeaks and Assange also lobbied the Trump administration to press Australia to appoint Assange as ambassador to the United States, a move that highlighted Assange's willingness to engage in political maneuvering for his personal benefit.

Cybersecurity experts attributed the hacking of the DNC server to the Russian government. Subsequently, 12

Russian GRU military intelligence agents were indicted for their involvement in the attack. The Senate Intelligence Committee's report stated that "WikiLeaks actively sought, and played, a key role in the Russian intelligence campaign and very likely knew it was assisting a Russian intelligence influence effort." According to the Mueller report, the Russian campaign used the pseudonym Guccifer 2.0 to share the hacked emails with WikiLeaks and other entities. The investigation also revealed communications between Guccifer 2.0 and WikiLeaks discussing the timing and nature of the document releases. When questioned about Guccifer 2.0's leaks, Assange remarked, "These look very much like they're from the Russians. But in some ways, they look very amateur, and almost look too much like the Russians."

Despite the mounting evidence of Russian involvement, Assange consistently denied that the Russian government was the source of the DNC and Podesta emails. He accused the Clinton campaign of engaging in a "kind of neo-

McCarthy hysteria" regarding Russian interference. On the eve of the election, Assange defended WikiLeaks' decision to publish the Clinton-related materials, stating that WikiLeaks publishes original documents "given to us if it is of political, diplomatic, historical or ethical importance." He emphasized that WikiLeaks had not received any original information on Donald Trump, Jill Stein, or Gary Johnson's campaigns.

Assange's actions during the 2016 election cycle had significant ramifications. The DNC email leak and the subsequent Podesta email releases fueled a media frenzy and deepened existing divisions within the Democratic Party. The revelations also played a crucial role in the broader narrative of foreign interference in the US electoral process, highlighting the vulnerabilities of political organizations to cyber attacks and the influential power of information warfare.

The fallout from these events underscored the complex interplay between journalism, political strategy, and international relations. Assange's involvement in the 2016 election saga was a testament to the contentious role that WikiLeaks and similar organizations play in modern political discourse. By releasing sensitive information at critical junctures, Assange positioned himself as both a champion of transparency and a controversial figure willing to manipulate the flow of information for strategic purposes.

In a July 2016 interview on Dutch television, Julian Assange made a controversial suggestion regarding the source of the Democratic National Committee (DNC) email leaks. He hinted that Seth Rich, a DNC staffer, might have been the source of the leaked emails and implied that Rich's murder was somehow connected to this leak. When the interviewer asked for clarification on whether Rich's killing was "simply a murder," Assange responded ambiguously, stating, "No. There's no finding. So, I'm suggesting that our sources take risks, and they become concerned to see things occurring like that."

Following these remarks, WikiLeaks offered a $20,000 reward for information about Rich's murder, emphasizing that they treat threats toward any suspected source with extreme seriousness. However, WikiLeaks also stated, "This should not be taken to imply that Seth Rich was a source to WikiLeaks or to imply that his murder is connected to our publications."

Assange's comments generated significant attention and fueled a conspiracy theory that had previously been confined to fringe parts of the internet. By mentioning Rich, Assange gave the theory a semblance of credibility, which led to a spike in public interest and speculation about the circumstances of Rich's death. This speculation distracted from the actual sources of the leaks and misled the public.

According to the Mueller investigation, Assange's suggestion that Rich was the source was false. The investigation found that Assange's implication was an attempt to obscure the true origin of the emails, which was Russian military intelligence. The investigation revealed that Assange had received the emails from Russian hackers after Rich had already been killed. Despite knowing this, Assange continued to coordinate with the Russian hackers to manage the release of the material.

Assange's actions and statements had far-reaching consequences. By linking Rich's murder to the DNC email leaks, Assange diverted attention from the real source of the leaks—Russian intelligence. This diversion played into the broader disinformation campaign orchestrated by Russia to disrupt the 2016 U.S. presidential election. The conspiracy theory around Seth Rich's murder served to muddy the waters and sow confusion among the public, which was precisely the outcome that Russian intelligence sought.

The manipulation of this narrative also highlighted the vulnerabilities inherent in the dissemination of information through platforms like WikiLeaks. While WikiLeaks purports to champion transparency and accountability, Assange's handling of the Seth Rich story illustrated how easily such platforms can be used to propagate false information and conspiracy theories. The ethical implications of these actions continue to be a subject of intense debate, raising questions about the responsibilities of those who manage and release sensitive information to the public.

Julian Assange's tenure in the Ecuadorian embassy was fraught with increasing tension and legal battles. On 19 October 2018, Assange filed a lawsuit against the Ecuadorian government, claiming that his fundamental rights and freedoms were being violated. He argued that Ecuador had threatened to revoke his protection, severely limited his access to the outside world, denied him visits from journalists and human rights organizations, and installed signal jammers to block his phone calls and internet access. Assange contended that these measures were oppressive and detrimental to his wellbeing.

However, an Ecuadorian judge dismissed Assange's claims. The court ruled that the requirements imposed on him, such as paying for his internet use and cleaning up after his cat, did not infringe on his right to asylum. This decision underscored the increasing strain in Assange's relationship with his host country, highlighting the challenges and discomforts of his prolonged stay within the embassy's confines.

In response to the escalating situation, on 21 December 2018, the United Nations Working Group on Arbitrary Detention urged the United Kingdom to allow Assange to leave the embassy freely. This call for action reflected growing international concern over Assange's prolonged detention and the conditions he faced. Despite these pleas, there was little immediate change in his circumstances.

Further international attention came in February 2019, when the parliament of Geneva passed a motion demanding that the Swiss government offer asylum to Assange. This motion indicated significant support for Assange's plight and an acknowledgment of the potential legal and human rights issues at play. Nonetheless, this move did not translate into immediate relief for Assange, who remained confined to the embassy.

In March 2019, Assange's legal team submitted a complaint to the Inter-American Commission on Human Rights. They requested that the Ecuadorian government ease the restrictive conditions imposed on Assange's residency at the embassy and sought protection from extradition to the United States. Additionally, they asked US prosecutors to unseal any criminal charges filed against Assange. However, the commission rejected this complaint, leaving Assange's situation unresolved.

Assange's legal and diplomatic battles illustrate the complex interplay between international law, human rights, and state sovereignty. His lawsuit against Ecuador and the subsequent rulings highlight the difficulties faced by individuals seeking asylum and protection from extradition, especially when accused of serious crimes. The international calls for his freedom underscore the broader concerns about the treatment of whistleblowers and the protection of press freedom in an increasingly digital world.

Throughout his time in the embassy, Assange's situation remained a focal point for debates on these issues. His case raised questions about the limits of asylum, the responsibilities of host countries, and the rights of individuals under international law. It also brought to light the sometimes precarious balance between national security interests and the protection of individual freedoms.

The legal proceedings against Assange and the responses from various international bodies reflect the contentious nature of his case. The UN Working Group on Arbitrary Detention's intervention and the Geneva parliament's motion both indicate significant international concern over Assange's treatment. These actions suggest a recognition of the potential human rights violations involved in his prolonged confinement and the importance of upholding international legal standards.

Despite these efforts, Assange's situation remained precarious. The Inter-American Commission on Human Rights' rejection of his complaint was a significant setback, demonstrating the challenges of seeking relief through international legal mechanisms. This decision underscored the difficulties faced by individuals in Assange's position, who must navigate a complex and often hostile legal landscape.

Assange's ongoing struggle highlights the broader issues at stake in cases involving whistleblowers and the dissemination of sensitive information. His situation exemplifies the risks faced by those who challenge powerful institutions and the potential repercussions of such actions. The legal and diplomatic battles surrounding Assange's asylum and potential extradition serve as a reminder of the contentious and often perilous nature of advocating for transparency and accountability in the modern world.

After Julian Assange was granted asylum and took refuge in the Ecuadorian embassy in London, extensive surveillance measures were put into place. The Ecuadorian security service hired UC Global, a private security firm, to manage security at the embassy. However, unbeknownst to the Ecuadorian officials, UC Global employees conducted detailed recordings of Assange's daily activities. These recordings included his interactions with embassy staff and visitors, including his legal team.

In December 2017, the surveillance efforts intensified with the installation of new CCTV cameras equipped with microphones. Microphones were also covertly installed in fire extinguishers, the women's bathroom, and various decorative items throughout the embassy. This covert surveillance operation was orchestrated by UC Global's director, who ensured that the United States Central Intelligence Agency (CIA) had direct access to the recordings.

The then-Ecuadorian ambassador to the UK, Juan Falconí Puig, remained unaware of this extensive surveillance operation until a bill for the services arrived at the embassy in May 2015. This prompted then-Ecuadorian foreign minister Ricardo Patiño to explain the situation to Ambassador Falconí. According to David Morales, UC Global's director, the surveillance had been authorized by a former Ecuadorian ambassador in London, Carlos Abad.

The full extent of the surveillance was revealed on 20 June 2019 by El Pais, which exposed the existence of recordings and reports about Assange made by UC Global. Following these revelations, Spain's High Court initiated an inquiry on

7 August 2019, after Assange filed a complaint. The complaint accused UC Global of violating his privacy and client-attorney privileges, as well as engaging in misappropriation, bribery, and money laundering.

Testimonies from former UC Global employees further implicated the firm in sharing surveillance materials with the CIA. These materials were reportedly handed over by a member of the security team of Sheldon Adelson, the owner of Las Vegas Sands. According to court documents reviewed by the Associated Press, Morales allegedly passed the recordings to Zohar Lahav, described as a security officer at Las Vegas Sands by Assange's lawyers.

The legal ramifications of this surveillance have been significant. In 2022, four associates of Assange filed a lawsuit against the CIA, alleging that their civil rights were violated through the recording of their conversations with Assange. This lawsuit, which claims violations of privacy and client-attorney privilege, marks a significant challenge to the actions of UC Global and the CIA.

In December 2023, a judge allowed the lawsuit to proceed, rejecting a CIA motion to dismiss the case. While some portions of the suit were dismissed, the core allegations were deemed substantial enough to move forward. This decision underscores the gravity of the allegations and the potential consequences for those involved in the unauthorized surveillance.

Assange's situation highlights the complex interplay between national security, legal rights, and personal privacy. The covert surveillance conducted by UC Global, allegedly at the behest of US intelligence, represents a significant breach of trust and raises serious ethical and legal questions. The recordings not only violated Assange's privacy but also compromised the confidentiality of his communications with his legal team, potentially undermining his right to a fair defense.

This episode also reflects broader concerns about the reach of intelligence agencies and their ability to conduct surveillance on individuals without their knowledge or consent. The involvement of the CIA and the alleged complicity of private security firms in such operations suggest a troubling trend towards the erosion of privacy rights in the name of national security.

As the legal battles surrounding this surveillance continue, they will likely set important precedents for the protection of privacy and the limits of government surveillance. The case against the CIA and UC Global will be closely watched, not only for its implications for Assange and his associates but also for its broader impact on the rights of individuals against intrusive and covert surveillance practices.

Chapter 6

Indictment and arrest

On 11 April 2019, Ecuador revoked Julian Assange's asylum, leading to his immediate arrest by the London Metropolitan Police for failing to appear in court. This marked a significant turning point in Assange's legal battles, as he was forcibly removed from the Ecuadorian Embassy where he had sought refuge for nearly seven years.

Following his arrest, the United States unsealed a previously hidden 2018 indictment against Assange, charging him with conspiracy to commit computer intrusion in connection with his collaboration with Chelsea Manning and the operations of WikiLeaks. This initial charge focused on

Assange's alleged role in assisting Manning in cracking a password to a classified U.S. government computer.

The legal pressures on Assange intensified on 23 May 2019, when a U.S. grand jury expanded the indictment, adding 17 new charges under the Espionage Act. These charges also stemmed from his involvement with Manning, significantly increasing the potential penalties Assange faced, now totaling 18 federal charges. The espionage charges were particularly contentious, as they brought into question the balance between national security and freedom of the press, given that Assange's actions were seen by many as journalistic activities.

On 25 June 2020, a new indictment was filed that broadened the scope of accusations against Assange. This indictment alleged that since 2009, Assange had attempted to recruit hackers and system administrators at various conferences worldwide. It also claimed that he conspired with hacking groups such as LulzSec and Anonymous. The indictment detailed how Assange and WikiLeaks allegedly supported Edward Snowden's escape from the United States and used Snowden's situation to further their recruitment efforts. Additionally, it accused WikiLeaks of exploiting a vulnerability in the United States Congress' system to access and publish Congressional Research Service reports.

Assange's defenders have consistently countered these U.S. accusations by portraying him as a journalist who merely published leaked information that embarrassed the U.S. government. They argue that Assange's work with WikiLeaks is no different from traditional investigative journalism that seeks to hold powerful entities accountable by exposing hidden truths.

The revocation of Assange's asylum and subsequent charges highlight the complexities and controversies surrounding his case. To many, Assange represents a figure who challenged government secrecy and advocated for transparency. His supporters argue that prosecuting him under the Espionage Act sets a dangerous precedent for press freedom, as it criminalizes the publication of classified information, a common practice in investigative journalism.

Assange's role in the release of classified documents through WikiLeaks has had far-reaching implications. WikiLeaks' publication of U.S. military and diplomatic cables in 2010, which included evidence of potential war crimes and diplomatic misconduct, brought global attention to issues of government transparency and accountability. Assange's defenders maintain that these disclosures were in the public interest and that punishing him for them would undermine the principles of a free press.

However, critics argue that Assange's actions went beyond journalism and entered the realm of criminal activity by actively assisting in the hacking of classified systems and endangering national security. They contend that his collaboration with hackers and the strategic release of sensitive information compromised the safety of individuals and national interests.

The legal battle over Assange's extradition to the United States continues to be a focal point of international debate. In the UK, his extradition proceedings have sparked protests and widespread calls for his release, with advocates arguing that extraditing him to the U.S. would subject him to an unfair trial and potential human rights violations.

The case also underscores the evolving nature of journalism in the digital age, where the lines between whistleblowing, hacking, and legitimate journalistic practices are increasingly blurred. Assange's use of digital platforms to disseminate classified information has raised important questions about the responsibilities and risks associated with modern journalism.

Chapter 7

Imprisonment in the UK

Following his arrest on 11 April 2019, Julian Assange was detained at HM Prison Belmarsh in London. This marked a pivotal moment in his contentious legal saga, shifting from the relative safety of the Ecuadorian Embassy to a high-security prison environment.

On 9 May 2019, Nils Melzer, the United Nations Special Rapporteur on Torture and Other Cruel, Inhuman or Degrading Treatment or Punishment, visited Assange in prison. Melzer reported that Assange exhibited symptoms typical of prolonged psychological torture, including extreme stress, chronic anxiety, and intense psychological trauma. Despite these findings, the British government expressed disagreement with some of Melzer's observations, indicating a contentious view of Assange's treatment and condition.

In a ruling on 13 September 2019, District Judge Vanessa Baraitser decided that Assange would not be released on 22 September, the end of his prison term for skipping bail, citing him as a flight risk. She emphasized that upon completing his sentence, Assange's status would transition from a serving prisoner to an individual facing extradition proceedings.

Melzer continued to voice concerns about Assange's health, stating on 1 November 2019 that his condition had worsened to the point of endangering his life. Melzer accused the UK government of failing to address these issues adequately. By the end of December 2019, Melzer had escalated his accusations, asserting that Assange's ongoing exposure to severe mental and emotional suffering amounted to psychological torture or other cruel, inhuman, or degrading treatment or punishment.

The situation drew international attention and advocacy, with Australian MPs Andrew Wilkie and George Christensen visiting Assange on 17 February 2020. They urged the UK and Australian governments to intervene and prevent his extradition to the United States. During this period, from November 2019 to February 2020, the medical community also expressed concerns about Assange's health and detention conditions, with numerous medical professionals signing petitions on his behalf.

On 25 March 2020, Assange's bid for bail was denied by Judge Baraitser, who dismissed his lawyers' argument that his imprisonment posed a high risk of contracting COVID-19. She highlighted Assange's history of taking extreme measures to avoid extradition as a factor in her decision.

Assange's life in HM Prison Belmarsh was harsh. Confined to his cell for 23 hours a day, with only one hour allocated for recreation indoors, his physical and mental health reportedly suffered. Writer Charles Glass visited Assange in December 2023 and noted his pale appearance. Assange shared with Glass that he had amassed a collection of 232 books during his time in prison, suggesting a continued engagement with intellectual pursuits despite the severe restrictions on his freedom.

Assange's incarceration at Belmarsh represents a significant chapter in his protracted legal battle and broader struggle against what he and his supporters perceive as unjust persecution for his role in WikiLeaks. The debate over his treatment and the implications for press freedom and human rights remains highly polarized. Critics argue that his detention conditions and the psychological toll it takes on him are disproportionate and amount to a form of punitive treatment. They contend that Assange's work with WikiLeaks, which involved publishing classified information, falls under the protection of journalistic activity and whistleblowing, essential for holding governments accountable.

On the other hand, authorities and detractors maintain that Assange's actions crossed the line into criminal conduct, especially concerning his alleged involvement in hacking activities and compromising national security. They argue that his extradition to the United States is justified to face charges that include conspiracy to commit computer intrusion and violations of the Espionage Act.

Assange's situation has sparked widespread debate on the balance between national security and the public's right to know. The potential extradition of a figure seen by many as a journalist raises concerns about the precedent it could set for press freedom and the protection of sources and whistleblowers. The legal and ethical complexities of Assange's case underscore the evolving challenges in a digital age where information dissemination and government transparency are increasingly at odds.

The international attention on Assange's health, treatment, and the legal proceedings against him highlights the broader implications for human rights and the responsibilities of states to ensure the humane treatment of detainees. As his legal battle continues, the outcome will likely have significant repercussions for the principles of justice, press freedom, and the protection of human rights defenders worldwide.

Chapter 8

Hearings on extradition to the

US

On 2 May 2019, the first hearing in London regarding the U.S. request for Julian Assange's extradition took place. When Judge Snow inquired if Assange consented to the extradition, Assange firmly replied, "I do not wish to surrender myself for extradition for doing journalism that has won many, many awards and protected many people." This declaration underscored his belief that his activities were rooted in journalistic principles and aimed at public interest.

By 13 June 2019, British Home Secretary Sajid Javid signed the extradition order, pushing the process forward despite

Assange's vehement objections and his legal team's efforts to contest it. This decision highlighted the UK government's alignment with the U.S. request, intensifying the legal drama surrounding Assange's fate.

Later in 2019, Judge Emma Arbuthnot, who had presided over several of Assange's extradition hearings, withdrew from the case. She cited a "perception of bias" due to reports about her family's connections to intelligence services and defense industries. This recusal aimed to preserve the integrity of the judicial process amid increasing scrutiny and concerns about impartiality. Vanessa Baraitser was subsequently appointed as the new presiding judge.

On 21 October 2019, during a case management hearing, Assange expressed his frustration with the proceedings. He remarked, "I don't understand how this is equitable. This superpower had 10 years to prepare for this case and I can't access my writings. It's very difficult where I am to do anything but these people have unlimited resources. They are saying journalists and whistleblowers are enemies of the people. They have unfair advantages dealing with documents. They [know] the interior of my life with my psychologist." His comments highlighted the significant disparities in resources and access between him and the U.S. government, as well as his perception of being unfairly targeted for his journalistic activities.

In February 2020, the court began hearing legal arguments. Assange's lawyers contended that he had been charged with political offenses and, therefore, could not be extradited. However, the hearings faced delays due to requests for additional time from both the prosecution and the defense, as well as the impact of the COVID-19 pandemic.

On 7 September 2020, Assange faced the espionage indictment with 18 counts in court. Judge Baraitser denied motions by Assange's legal team to dismiss the new charges or to adjourn the hearing for better preparation. During the hearing, Assange interrupted the U.S. government's lawyer, shouting, "This is nonsense," which led Judge Baraitser to warn him that further interruptions could result in his expulsion from the courtroom.

Witnesses testified remotely due to COVID-19 restrictions, causing technical delays. Among the witnesses was Daniel Ellsberg, and torture victim Khaled el-Masri, whose testimony was reduced to a written statement. Other witnesses testified about the conditions of Assange's imprisonment, which they argued would likely worsen if he were extradited to the U.S., placing him at a high risk of depression and suicide, exacerbated by his Asperger syndrome. The defense also highlighted a prison service report stating that a hidden razor blade had been found in Assange's cell, and revealed that Assange had contacted the Samaritans phone service on numerous occasions. A forensic psychiatrist for the prosecution, however, claimed that Assange's risk of suicide was manageable and described his symptoms as "self-dramatising or hyperbolic."

Patrick Eller, a former forensics examiner with the U.S. Army Criminal Investigation Command, testified that Assange did not crack and could not have cracked the password mentioned in the U.S. indictment. According to Eller, Chelsea Manning had intentionally sent only a portion of the password's hash. He also noted that password cracking was a common topic among soldiers at Forward Operating Base Hammer, suggesting that Manning's message was unrelated to the classified documents already in her possession.

On 30 September 2020, new allegations surfaced about the surveillance of the Ecuadorian embassy by UC Global. A former UC Global employee, speaking anonymously for fear of reprisals, revealed that the firm had conducted "an increasingly sophisticated operation" after being connected with the Trump administration by Sheldon Adelson. Intelligence agents allegedly discussed plans to break into the embassy to kidnap or poison Assange and attempted to obtain the DNA of a baby believed to be Assange's child.

On 4 January 2021, Judge Baraitser ruled that Assange could not be extradited to the United States, citing concerns about his mental health and the risk of suicide in a U.S. prison. While she sided with the U.S. on other points, including whether the charges constituted political offenses and whether Assange was entitled to freedom of speech protections, the ruling on his mental health was pivotal. It emphasized the grave risk to Assange's well-being if extradited, thus halting the immediate threat of his transfer to the U.S.

These proceedings highlighted the complex intersection of international law, human rights, and press freedom. Assange's case remains a contentious symbol in the ongoing debate over the role of journalism in holding powerful entities accountable and the protections afforded to those who expose governmental secrets. The outcome of this legal battle will likely have significant implications for the future of investigative journalism, whistleblower protections, and the broader discourse on state transparency and accountability.

In the ongoing legal saga of Julian Assange, significant developments occurred in early 2022 when the case was remitted to Westminster Magistrates' Court with the directive that it be sent to Home Secretary Priti Patel for the final decision on whether to extradite Assange to the United States. The court's decision came after the presiding judge acknowledged that if the assurances provided by the U.S. had been presented earlier, it might have altered her decision regarding Assange's extradition. On 24 January 2022, Assange was granted permission to petition the Supreme Court of the United Kingdom for an appeal hearing. However, in March 2022, the court refused to allow the appeal, stating that Assange had not raised an arguable point of law.

On 20 April 2022, Chief Magistrate Paul Goldspring of the Westminster Magistrates' Court formally approved the extradition of Assange to the United States and referred the decision to Home Secretary Priti Patel. On 17 June 2022, Patel approved the extradition, moving Assange closer to being sent to the U.S. to face charges.

Following Patel's approval, on 1 July 2022, Assange lodged an appeal against the extradition in the High Court. On 22 August 2022, his legal team submitted a Perfected Grounds of Appeal before the High Court, challenging District Judge Vanessa Baraitser's decision from 4 January 2021 with new evidence. Assange also made an additional appeal to the European Court of Human Rights, but on 13 December 2022, this appeal was declared inadmissible.

In April 2023, European unions and associations of journalists from various countries, including Portugal, Armenia, Great Britain, and Greece, granted Assange honorary membership. The European Federation of Journalists (EFJ) and its affiliates joined the International Federation of Journalists (IFJ) in appealing to U.S. and UK authorities to release Assange and drop all charges against him. The EFJ expressed concerns about the impact of Assange's continued detention on media freedom and the rights of journalists globally and urged European governments to work towards securing his release. In May 2023, Assange wrote a letter to King Charles III, describing himself as a political prisoner and requesting the King visit him in prison.

In May 2023, Assange's lawyers indicated they were open to negotiating a plea deal, but maintained that "no crime has been committed and the facts involved in the case don't support a crime." Meanwhile, in June 2023, it was reported that the FBI was seeking to gather new evidence in the case. The FBI had requested to interview journalist Andrew O'Hagan, who refused to provide a witness statement against Assange, citing solidarity with a fellow journalist.

On 6 June 2023, the High Court in London dismissed Assange's appeal. Justice Jonathan Swift ruled that "none of the four grounds of appeal raises any properly arguable point." In a second ruling, Justice Swift denied Assange permission to challenge a January 2021 ruling by Judge Baraitser.

A two-day hearing in the High Court began on 20 February 2024, but Assange was too ill to attend. His legal team requested leave to appeal the extradition order signed by Home Secretary Patel in 2022. On 26 March, the judges issued a written judgment that was not a final decision. They sought assurances from the U.S. government that Assange would be able to avail himself of the First Amendment, would not be prejudiced by his nationality, and that the death penalty would not be imposed. The court stipulated that if these assurances were not provided, Assange would be given leave to appeal.

On 16 April, the U.S. Embassy in London provided a diplomatic note assuring that Assange "will not be prejudiced by reason of his nationality with respect to which defenses he may seek to raise at trial and at sentencing"; that "a sentence of death will neither be sought nor imposed"; and that Assange had "the ability to raise and seek to rely upon" the First Amendment, although its applicability "is exclusively within the purview of the U.S. courts." Stella Assange, Julian's partner, commented on this saying, "The United States has issued a non-assurance in relation to the First Amendment, and a standard assurance in relation to the death penalty."

On 20 May, the two High Court judges, Dame Victoria Sharp and Sir Jeremy Johnson, found that the assurances regarding the First Amendment and the nationality question were insufficient. Consequently, they granted Assange leave to appeal against his extradition. This decision highlighted the ongoing complexities and contentious issues surrounding Assange's case, particularly concerning the legal protections he might or might not receive under U.S. law.

Throughout this tumultuous period, Assange's supporters have continuously argued that his work with WikiLeaks constitutes journalism and that his prosecution sets a dangerous precedent for press freedom. They contend that Assange's actions in publishing classified materials exposed significant government malfeasance and were in the public interest. Conversely, his critics argue that his disclosures endangered lives and compromised national security, portraying him as a reckless individual rather than a crusader for transparency.

The case has drawn international attention, with numerous human rights organizations, media groups, and political figures weighing in on the potential ramifications of Assange's extradition. The prospect of Assange facing trial in the U.S. raises critical questions about the extent to which journalists and publishers can be held accountable for disseminating information that governments seek to keep secret.

As the legal proceedings continue, Assange remains a polarizing figure, emblematic of the broader debates over state secrecy, the role of whistleblowers, and the limits of journalistic freedom. His case serves as a litmus test for the balance between national security interests and the fundamental principles of a free press.

The outcome of Assange's legal battles will undoubtedly have far-reaching implications for journalists and whistleblowers worldwide. It will either reinforce or challenge the boundaries of legal protections for those who seek to expose governmental misconduct. Moreover, it will shape the future landscape of investigative journalism, influencing how sensitive information is handled and published in the digital age.

Julian Assange's legal battles have drawn a mixture of reactions, from support among some American journalism institutions and bipartisan politicians, to widespread condemnation by various non-government organizations and activists who view his potential extradition as a significant threat to press freedom.

In 2019, The New York Times' Editorial Board voiced concern over Assange's prosecution. They acknowledged the administration's initial charge against Assange was legally sound but warned that the prosecution could escalate into an attack on the First Amendment, particularly given the administration's antagonistic stance toward the press, labeling it "the enemy of the people." Kenneth Roth, executive director of Human Rights Watch, echoed these concerns, stating that Britain's decision on Assange's extradition was a critical barrier preventing a major threat to global media freedom. Reporters Without Borders also urged the UK to reject the extradition request, arguing that complying would set a dangerous precedent for journalists, whistleblowers, and their sources worldwide.

In March 2020, the International Bar Association's Human Rights Institute (IBAHRI) condemned the mistreatment of

Assange during his extradition trial, highlighting concerns over due process and fair treatment. By September of the same year, an open letter supporting Assange was addressed to then-Prime Minister Boris Johnson, signed by the Presidents of Argentina and Venezuela, along with approximately 160 other politicians. This letter emphasized the broad political opposition to Assange's extradition. In October 2020, U.S. Representatives Tulsi Gabbard and Thomas Massie introduced a bipartisan resolution opposing Assange's extradition, underscoring the issue's contentious nature within the American political landscape.

The German human rights commissioner, Bärbel Kofler, in December 2020, urged the UK to consider Assange's physical and mental health before making a final decision on his extradition. This plea was reinforced by Nils Melzer, the UN special rapporteur on torture, who called for Assange's immediate release, citing his prolonged arbitrary detention over the past decade.

Assange's legal defense received substantial financial support in 2022 through an innovative auction of non-fungible tokens (NFTs). An artwork titled "Clock," created by Pak in collaboration with Assange, was sold to AssangeDAO, a decentralized autonomous organization of over 10,000 supporters. The NFT raised 16,593 ether (approximately $52.8 million at the time), providing significant funds for Assange's legal efforts. The "Clock" NFT updates daily to reflect the duration of Assange's imprisonment, serving as a powerful visual reminder of his ongoing plight.

In 2024, The Guardian expressed its opposition to Assange's extradition, stating that it was crucial not only for his freedom but for the broader principle of journalistic independence. The Guardian described the extradition attempt as a "pernicious threat to journalism" with far-reaching global implications. Amnesty International's Simon Crowther also warned that extraditing Assange to the U.S. would compel journalists worldwide to constantly look over their shoulders, fearing similar repercussions.

Political rallies supporting Assange have taken place in major cities such as London, Rome, Brussels, and Berlin, demonstrating significant public opposition to his extradition. On 4 March 2024, while Assange's appeal was being considered by the High Court, German Chancellor Olaf Scholz remarked that it would be beneficial for the British courts to provide Assange with the necessary protection, reflecting international concern over his potential extradition.

Assange's case continues to be a flashpoint in the debate over press freedom, state secrecy, and the rights of whistleblowers. His supporters argue that his work with WikiLeaks represents legitimate journalism that exposed critical government misconduct and served the public interest. Conversely, critics contend that his actions endangered lives and compromised national security, portraying him as reckless rather than a defender of transparency.

The outcome of Assange's legal battles will have profound implications for journalists and whistleblowers globally. A decision to extradite could set a dangerous precedent, potentially stifling investigative journalism and deterring the publication of sensitive information that holds governments accountable. On the other hand, a decision to release Assange could reaffirm the importance of press freedom and the protections afforded to those who expose wrongdoing.

Chapter 9

Plea bargain and release

On the evening following a significant development in Julian Assange's legal situation, his representatives Jennifer Robinson and Barry Pollack held a press conference attended by numerous current Australian politicians. Former senior Australian diplomat and international relations expert Ian Kemish described the consular assistance provided by Australia as unparalleled, albeit delayed. He noted that multiple successive Australian governments had been slow to provide this extraordinary level of support.

The Australian government required Assange to repay the costs of the charter flight for his transfer from the United Kingdom to Saipan and then to Australia, as he was barred from flying on commercial airlines. The total amount requested for this charter flight was US$520,000.

Charlie Savage of The New York Times highlighted that this situation marks the first instance where the U.S. has charged a non-governmental official with publishing secret documents. This has raised significant concerns among press freedom organizations, which warn that this could set a dangerous precedent for journalism. Jameel Jaffer, executive director of the Knight First Amendment Institute at Columbia University, pointed out that the plea deal "would avert the worst-case scenario for press freedom, but this deal contemplates that Assange will have served five years in prison for activities that journalists engage in every day." He added that such a deal would cast a long shadow over the most critical forms of journalism, not just in the U.S., but globally.

Julian Assange, the founder of WikiLeaks, has been at the center of a protracted legal battle that has significant implications for press freedom and the rights of whistleblowers. WikiLeaks gained notoriety for publishing classified documents that exposed government misconduct and controversial military operations. Assange's supporters argue that his work represents legitimate journalism that holds powerful institutions accountable, while his detractors claim that his actions endangered lives and compromised national security.

The legal proceedings against Assange have sparked a global debate about the boundaries of journalistic freedom, the role of whistleblowers, and the extent to which governments can exert control over information dissemination. The U.S. government's decision to charge Assange with publishing classified documents has been particularly contentious, as it challenges the traditional protections afforded to journalists under the First Amendment.

Assange's case raises several critical legal and ethical questions. One of the central issues is whether the act of publishing classified information, which is a common journalistic practice, can be criminalized without infringing on press freedom. Many journalists and legal experts fear that prosecuting Assange sets a precedent that could deter investigative journalism and restrict the flow of information that is vital for public accountability.

Moreover, the conditions of Assange's detention and the legal strategies employed by his defense team have been subjects of intense scrutiny. Assange's health and well-being have been a persistent concern, with various human rights organizations and medical professionals advocating for his humane treatment. The protracted nature of his legal battle has also highlighted the need for more robust international protections for journalists and whistleblowers who expose government wrongdoing.

Assange's situation has elicited strong reactions from the international community. Various governments, human rights organizations, and press freedom advocates have called for his release and condemned the actions taken against him. In Australia, his home country, the government's response has been mixed. While there has been substantial diplomatic support for Assange, critics argue that the assistance has been inconsistent and delayed.

The diplomatic efforts to secure Assange's release have involved complex negotiations and considerable political pressure. The Australian government's decision to require Assange to repay the costs of his charter flight reflects the broader challenges in providing consular assistance to citizens involved in high-profile legal cases abroad. Despite these challenges, there has been a growing consensus among Australian politicians and diplomats that more decisive action is needed to protect Assange's rights and secure his safe return.

The outcome of Assange's case will have far-reaching implications for press freedom and the protection of journalists worldwide. If Assange is ultimately convicted and imprisoned for publishing classified information, it could create a chilling effect on investigative journalism, discouraging reporters from pursuing stories that involve government secrets or sensitive information. This could undermine the media's role as a watchdog and reduce the public's access to information that is crucial for democratic governance.

Conversely, if Assange is acquitted or if the charges are dropped, it could reinforce the principle that journalists have the right to publish information in the public interest, even if it involves classified documents. Such a precedent would strengthen the protections for journalists and whistleblowers, ensuring that they can continue to hold powerful institutions accountable without fear of retribution.

Chapter 10

Written works, television show, and views

In his 2012 book Cypherpunks: Freedom and the Future of the Internet, Julian Assange articulated his core belief: "the traditional cypherpunk juxtaposition ... privacy for the weak, transparency for the powerful." This principle underscores Assange's advocacy for encryption as a vital tool for protecting individuals against the invasive scrutiny of governments, corporations, and surveillance agencies. He also views encryption as a means for states to shield themselves from Western imperialism. Assange's stance is rooted in the cypherpunk movement, which promotes the use of cryptographic techniques to foster privacy and security in the digital age.

In 2012, Assange expanded his reach by hosting the World Tomorrow show, broadcast by the Russian network RT. This platform allowed him to further discuss his ideas on freedom, privacy, and transparency. Assange has penned several notable works, including "State and Terrorist Conspiracies" (2006), "Conspiracy as Governance" (2006), "The Hidden Curse of Thomas Paine" (2008), "What's New About WikiLeaks?" (2011), and the foreword to Cypherpunks (2012). He also contributed research to Suelette Dreyfus's Underground (1997) and received a co-writer credit for the Calle 13 song "Multi Viral" (2013).

Assange's political views are complex and often controversial. In 2010, he identified as a libertarian, stating that "WikiLeaks is designed to make capitalism more free and ethical" and to expose injustice, not to remain neutral. By 2013, he claimed to be the "number three" hacker in the world. In 2017, Assange asserted that WikiLeaks had a perfect record, contrasting this with what he described as the credibility of only 2% of mainstream journalists.

In 2010, Assange secured a lucrative deal for his autobiography worth at least US$1.3 million. However, the publication of Julian Assange, The Unauthorised Autobiography by Canongate Books in 2011 was fraught with controversy. Assange immediately disavowed the book, accusing Canongate of breaching their contract by publishing a draft he considered to be a mere "narrative and literary interpretation of a conversation between the writer and me." He further criticized the draft as "a work in progress" and "entirely uncorrected or fact-checked by me."

In 2014, Andrew O'Hagan, who had been Assange's ghostwriter, shared his experience, noting that "the story of his life mortified him and sent him scurrying for excuses." O'Hagan recalled that Assange never truly wanted to write the book. Colin Robinson, co-publisher of Assange's 2012 book Cypherpunks, criticized O'Hagan for focusing on Assange's character defects rather than the larger issues Assange had been raising. Robinson argued that O'Hagan's piece inadvertently served the same purpose as an organized smear campaign against Assange.

Assange's book When Google Met WikiLeaks was published by OR Books in 2014. It details a meeting requested by Google CEO Eric Schmidt, who visited Assange while he was on bail in rural Norfolk, UK. Schmidt was accompanied by Jared Cohen, Scott Malcomson, and Lisa Shields, vice-president of the Council on Foreign Relations. Excerpts from the book were published on the Newsweek website, and Assange participated in a Q&A session on Reddit to promote the book.

Assange's interactions with the media have often been contentious. In 2011, an article in Private Eye by its editor, Ian Hislop, recounted a phone call from Assange, who was angry about a report that Israel Shamir, an Assange associate in Russia, was a Holocaust denier. According to Hislop, Assange suggested that British journalists, including the editor of The Guardian, were involved in a Jewish-led conspiracy to smear WikiLeaks. Assange denied these allegations, stating that Hislop had "distorted, invented or misremembered almost every significant claim and phrase." He emphasized WikiLeaks' support from diverse groups, including Jewish supporters and pan-Arab democracy activists, all united by a shared hope for a just world.

Assange's influence and the controversies surrounding him extend beyond his writings and media appearances. His legal battles and the global debate over his actions have highlighted crucial issues about freedom of information, the role of whistleblowers, and the limits of governmental power. Assange's supporters argue that his work with WikiLeaks represents legitimate journalism that holds powerful institutions accountable. They believe that prosecuting Assange for publishing classified documents sets a dangerous precedent that could deter investigative journalism and restrict the public's access to important information.

On the other hand, Assange's detractors contend that his actions endangered lives and compromised national security. They argue that the indiscriminate release of sensitive information, without regard for the potential harm it could cause, goes beyond the bounds of responsible journalism. This debate touches on the broader ethical and legal questions about the balance between transparency and security, and the responsibilities of journalists in the digital age.

The legal proceedings against Assange have also underscored the need for stronger international protections for journalists and whistleblowers. Assange's prolonged detention and the conditions of his imprisonment have been criticized by various human rights organizations and medical professionals. They have called for his humane treatment and highlighted the impact of his case on press freedom worldwide.

As Assange's case continues to unfold, its implications for journalism and democracy remain profound. The outcome will likely influence how governments handle similar cases in the future and shape the legal landscape for whistleblowers and journalists who expose government misconduct. If Assange is convicted, it could create a chilling effect on investigative journalism, discouraging reporters from pursuing stories that involve classified information. Conversely, if Assange is acquitted or the charges are dropped, it could reinforce the protections for journalists and affirm the principle that publishing information in the public interest is a vital component of a free and democratic society.

Chapter 11

Personal life

As a teenager, Julian Assange married Teresa, who was also in her teens, and in 1989, they welcomed their son, Daniel. However, their relationship became strained, leading to their separation and a prolonged custody battle over Daniel that lasted until 1999. This tumultuous period took a toll on Assange, with his mother noting that his brown hair turned white during the custody dispute, a testament to the immense stress he endured.

In 2006, Assange ventured into online dating, creating a profile on OkCupid under the username Harry Harrison. In this profile, he described himself as a "passionate, and often pig-headed activist intellectual" engaged in a "consuming, dangerous human rights project." He was candid about seeking a "siren for [a] love affair, children, and occasional criminal conspiracy." This profile, verified by OkCupid CEO Sam Yagan, was last accessed in December 2006, offering a glimpse into Assange's personal aspirations and self-perception during that time.

Daniel Domscheit-Berg, in his 2011 memoir Inside WikiLeaks, mentioned that Assange had claimed to have fathered several children. This was corroborated by an email from Assange in January 2007, where he mentioned having a daughter. Further revelations came in 2015 when Assange, in an open letter to French President François Hollande, disclosed that he had another child. He stated that this child, his youngest, was French, as was the child's mother. Assange expressed that his family had been subjected to death threats and harassment due to his work, forcing them to change their identities and limit contact with him.

In 2015, Assange began a relationship with Stella Moris, his lawyer. Their relationship deepened over time, leading to their engagement in 2017. The couple has two sons, born in

2017 and 2019. Stella Moris revealed their relationship in 2020, driven by fears for Assange's life amid his legal and political battles. The revelation highlighted the personal sacrifices and risks associated with Assange's work and his ongoing legal struggles.

On 7 November 2021, Julian and Stella Assange announced their intention to take legal action against Deputy UK Prime Minister Dominic Raab and Jenny Louis, the governor of Belmarsh Prison. They accused Raab and Louis of violating their human rights by obstructing and delaying their marriage. The prison service later granted them permission to marry, and on 23 March 2022, the couple tied the knot in Belmarsh Prison. This marriage, conducted under such unusual and challenging circumstances, underscored the relentless pressure and scrutiny faced by Assange and his family.

Julian Assange's familial connections extend to his cousin, Kylie Moore-Gilbert, an Australian-British academic and former Iranian hostage. This connection adds another layer to Assange's complex personal narrative, intertwining his story with broader themes of political struggle and resilience.

Assange's life has been a labyrinth of personal and professional challenges. His early marriage to Teresa and the subsequent custody battle over their son Daniel marked the beginning of a life fraught with conflict and controversy. The intense stress from this period manifested physically, as noted by his mother, who observed his hair turning white.

His foray into online dating in 2006 through OkCupid, where he described himself with a mix of idealism and defiance, paints a picture of a man deeply committed to his cause yet yearning for personal connections. The verification of his profile by OkCupid CEO Sam Yagan adds a layer of authenticity to this glimpse into Assange's personal life.

Daniel Domscheit-Berg's memoir, Inside WikiLeaks, reveals that Assange claimed to have multiple children, adding to the intrigue surrounding his personal life. Assange's email in 2007 mentioning a daughter and his 2015 open letter to French President Hollande about another child highlight the complexities and dangers his family faced due to his activism. The threats and harassment forced them to adopt new identities and maintain a low profile, reflecting the severe consequences of Assange's work.

Assange's relationship with Stella Moris, his lawyer, further humanizes his story. Their engagement and the birth of their two sons in 2017 and 2019, respectively, show a man who, despite his tumultuous life, found love and built a family. Stella's decision to go public with their relationship in 2020, motivated by concerns for Assange's safety, underscores the perilous nature of his situation.

The couple's legal battle to marry within Belmarsh Prison, culminating in their wedding on 23 March 2022, is a testament to their determination and love. This union, forged in the shadow of legal and political adversity, highlights the human side of Assange's high-profile struggles.

Assange's connection to Kylie Moore-Gilbert, an Australian-British academic who endured captivity in Iran, adds another dimension to his narrative. It connects his personal story to broader geopolitical issues and the resilience required to navigate such challenges.

Chapter 12

Commentary about Assange

Public figures, including journalists, whistleblowers, activists, and world leaders, have expressed a wide range of opinions on Julian Assange. These views span from high praise for his contributions to free speech to extreme calls for his execution. Many journalists and advocates for free expression have commended Assange for his dedication to exposing hidden truths and protecting freedom of the press. His work, particularly through WikiLeaks, has been seen as a bold challenge to government and corporate secrecy, pushing the boundaries of what the public has a right to know.

On the other hand, Assange has faced criticism from former colleagues who have questioned his work ethic, editorial decisions, and personality. Some argue that his approach to whistleblowing and the release of sensitive information is reckless. These criticisms extend beyond his work habits and into debates about his broader motivations, especially following the 2016 U.S. presidential election. His role in the release of emails from the Democratic National Committee sparked widespread speculation about his potential ties to Russia, leading to questions about whether he was acting as a neutral journalist or as a political player with ulterior motives.

The controversy surrounding Assange intensified after his arrest in 2019. A significant point of contention among journalists and commentators was whether Assange should be considered a journalist. His supporters point to his numerous journalism awards, including the prestigious Walkley Award, Australia's national prize for journalism, as evidence of his status as a journalist. His contributions to investigative journalism, particularly in exposing war crimes and government misconduct, have earned him accolades from those who see his work as a vital check on unchecked power.

However, critics argue that Assange's actions go far beyond those of a traditional journalist. The U.S. government has accused him of not merely gathering information but actively soliciting, stealing, and indiscriminately publishing classified government documents. They contend that his actions put lives at risk and compromised national security. This view suggests that Assange's methods cross ethical boundaries, placing him in a different category from investigative reporters who work within certain legal and professional norms.

In 2024, Assange's legal team continued to defend his work, describing him as a journalist who courageously exposed U.S. military wrongdoing in Iraq and Afghanistan. They maintained that Assange's publications were in the public interest, shedding light on government activities that would otherwise remain hidden. His defenders argue that punishing Assange for these revelations threatens not only his freedom but also the freedom of the press worldwide. They warn that prosecuting Assange sets a dangerous precedent, whereby journalists and whistleblowers could be criminalized for holding governments accountable.

The U.S. government, however, has remained firm in its stance that Assange's activities cannot be considered journalism. They emphasize that his indiscriminate publication of classified documents went far beyond the responsible journalism that informs the public without endangering lives. For the U.S., this case is about safeguarding national security and ensuring that classified information is not used recklessly to undermine governmental operations.

The ongoing debate over Assange's role highlights the complex intersection between journalism, whistleblowing, and national security. For some, Assange is a hero who exposed corruption and military wrongdoing. For others, he is a reckless figure whose actions have endangered lives and compromised the security of nations. The legal and ethical discussions surrounding Assange will likely have lasting implications for the future of journalism, particularly in how governments and the press navigate the delicate balance between transparency and security.

Chapter 13

Reflection questions

How do you perceive Julian Assange's actions in the context of whistleblowing—do you believe they serve the greater good or cross ethical boundaries?

_____

_____

_____

_____

What role should transparency play in government and military affairs, and where should the line be drawn for national security?

_____

_____

_____

_____

In what ways has Assange's work with WikiLeaks influenced public perception of journalism and the responsibility of the press?

_____

How do Assange's actions challenge traditional definitions of journalism? Should his methods be considered part of investigative reporting?

Do you believe whistleblowers like Assange are essential to maintaining accountability in government and corporate institutions? Why or why not?

How does Assange's personal journey, from his early activism to his global notoriety, shape your view of him as an individual?

What do you think are the long-term implications of Assange's case for the freedom of the press and free speech worldwide?

How do you balance the need for government secrecy with the public's right to know about unethical or illegal activities?

To what extent should governments be allowed to prosecute individuals who publish classified information? Should whistleblowers be protected under the law?

What responsibility, if any, do platforms like WikiLeaks have for the potential consequences of releasing sensitive information?

In what ways did Assange's decisions impact not only governments but also the lives of individuals featured in the leaks? How should accountability be managed in such cases?

How does Assange's struggle with various governments over the years affect your understanding of global power dynamics?

_____

_____

_____

_____

What lessons can we learn from the way different countries, including the U.S., UK, and Australia, have handled the Assange case?

_____

_____

_____

_____

How does Assange's life reflect broader tensions between activism and personal sacrifice? To what extent should activists be willing to endure such consequences?

_____

_____

_____

Do you believe Julian Assange's work represents a fight for justice, or do his actions undermine the very systems meant to protect society? Why?

Chapter 14

Lessons learned

The Power of Transparency: Assange's work through WikiLeaks demonstrated how transparency can hold powerful institutions accountable, exposing hidden truths that can affect the public's understanding of governments and corporations.

The Importance of Freedom of Speech: Assange's life underscores the significance of free speech in a democratic society, particularly the role of journalism in bringing light to matters of public interest.

Ethical Complexities in Whistleblowing: Assange's actions highlight the ethical dilemmas involved in whistleblowing. It teaches us that while exposing wrongdoing is important, it must be balanced with concerns about privacy and national security.

The Consequences of Defiance: Assange's story reveals the personal and legal consequences of standing up to powerful governments and institutions, showing the immense pressures faced by whistleblowers and activists.

Persistence in the Face of Adversity: Despite numerous legal battles, threats, and years of confinement, Assange has remained committed to his cause, teaching us the value of persistence and determination.

The Global Impact of Information: Assange's life illustrates how the dissemination of information can have far-reaching consequences beyond national borders, influencing global politics and international relations.

The Risks of Radical Transparency: While transparency is important, Assange's case shows the potential dangers of releasing information indiscriminately, including harm to individuals and national security concerns.

Complexity of Justice: Assange's legal battles teach us that justice is not always clear-cut. His case raises questions about whether he is a hero for truth or a criminal, showing how legal systems can be used to pursue political agendas.

The Role of Technology in Activism: Through WikiLeaks, Assange used digital platforms to challenge traditional power structures, demonstrating the transformative power of technology in modern activism.

Personal Sacrifice for a Cause: Assange's life teaches that pursuing a cause with conviction often requires personal sacrifice. His long-standing commitment to WikiLeaks came at the cost of his personal freedom and relationships.

Public Perception Can Shift Quickly: Assange's life story shows how public opinion can change dramatically. Initially hailed as a hero, his reputation shifted as controversies arose, revealing how narratives can evolve.

The Fragility of Press Freedom: Assange's legal struggles reflect the vulnerability of press freedom, even in democratic societies, showing how governments can challenge the work of journalists in the name of national security.

Moral Ambiguity in Leadership: Assange's leadership of WikiLeaks teaches that even those with noble causes can face moral ambiguity in their methods, particularly when the release of information has unintended negative consequences.

Collaboration and Conflict: Assange's relationships with journalists, whistleblowers, and activists reveal the importance of collaboration in advocacy but also highlight the conflicts that can arise when visions diverge.

The Power of Ideas to Influence Change: Ultimately, Assange's life teaches us that ideas—whether they challenge authority or advocate for transparency—can inspire movements, provoke debate, and push society towards change.

Conclusion

In conclusion, the life and work of Julian Assange represent a journey filled with complexity, controversy, and conviction. Through this book, we've delved into the man behind WikiLeaks, exploring not just his triumphs and achievements but also the challenges and personal sacrifices he endured. His relentless pursuit of truth, transparency, and accountability has sparked global discussions on the ethics of whistleblowing, the role of journalism, and the balance between privacy and free speech.

As readers, your commitment to understanding Assange's life and the wider implications of his work is invaluable. It's your curiosity, engagement, and willingness to seek out these stories that give power and meaning to this book. Without your investment of time and resources, these pages would be just that – mere words on paper. But your involvement transforms this biography into something alive, something capable of sparking reflection, debate, and change. Your decision to read this book is not just a testament to your interest in Assange but also to your desire to question the status quo, to dig deeper into issues that shape our world today.

We've examined Assange's ideals on transparency and accountability, how his work challenged the global power structure, and the personal toll his convictions took on him. His journey, filled with legal battles and political persecution, teaches us about the price of defiance and the importance of persistence. You, as a reader, have walked this path alongside him through these chapters, and I hope you've found the experience both enlightening and thought-provoking.

This book is not just a story about one man's life; it's a reflection of the broader questions facing our society today – the role of journalism, the power of information, and the ethical responsibilities we hold. By engaging with this biography, you've contributed to a much-needed dialogue about these essential topics. And for that, I want to sincerely thank you.

Your support as a reader is what brings life to this work. Without your participation, this book wouldn't be able to fulfill its purpose: to inform, challenge, and inspire. It's your engagement that keeps the story of Julian Assange relevant and meaningful, long after you've turned the final page.

If you found this book insightful, if it provoked thought or stirred your emotions in any way, I humbly ask for your continued support in the form of a positive review. Reviews play a crucial role in helping others discover this work, and your words could make all the difference. By sharing your thoughts and reflections, you're not only supporting the book but also helping to keep the conversations sparked by Assange's life alive. Your review can help inspire more readers to dive into these important discussions.

Once again, I truly appreciate the time, attention, and resources you've dedicated to reading this biography. I hope it leaves you with a deeper understanding of Julian Assange's life, as well as a renewed curiosity about the power of information and the role we all play in shaping the world around us.

Thank you for being part of this journey, and for your continued support. Together, we can ensure that these important stories, lessons, and debates continue to be shared and discussed.

Printed in Great Britain
by Amazon